I0140216

VOICE OF SENEMAI

a Collection of Poems

Vagi Samuel Jnr.

jdt
Publications

Published by JDT Publications
Port Moresby, National Capital District, Papua New Guinea
Email: jdtpublications@gmail.com

National Library of Papua New Guinea
Cataloguing-in-Publication entry:

Samuel, Vagi Jnr. 1986 — .
    Voice of Senemai: A Collection of Poems.

ISBN-13: 978-9980-901-72-9

1. Papua New Guinea poetry. 2. Poetry
    i. JDT Publications   ii. Title
PNG/821/S25 – dc22

Printed in USA by CreateSpace Independent Publishing.

To my father, Samuel Vagi and mother, Elsie Vagi, you both are the inspiration and motivation that propelled me in this endeavor. I thank you for your love, care and support behind me all through the years.

Vagi Samuel Jnr.

Big thanks to Jordan Dean,
a passionate Papuan New Guinean writer who generously assisted me in getting this book reviewed and published. I am also thankful for his support and encouragement in assisting other fellow aspiring writers to have their works published.

To Raymond Boga-Lohia, my big brother for being a blessing. You taught me to be a great thinker, a wise advisor and a gentle leader within any means. It is also fitting that I acknowledge your spiritual and professional leadership upon my life.

Thank you Kaka Ray!

PROLOGUE

The world around us is changing at a rapid pace and for us as a small nation like Papua New Guinea we are caught up in this trend. Our villages are changing so as our communities and societies. There are so many factors amongst others that derail our progress and detour us from realizing our full potential as individuals and as a nation.

Hence, there are three things that have dawned on me that I think are the brands that cause perceived changes around us. In no order of importance, they are dependency, jealousy and complacency. When can we be able to resist the transient ways of counter productivity? Do we hear ourselves in the clutters and calamities of these trying times?

'Voice of Senemai' is not merely a remedy; it is a calling that comes from everyday experiences. It is a collection of poems and prose that captures how an ordinary Papua New Guinean can be able to share dreams and imaginations, pains and sufferings, hunger and thirst, issues and strife, love and shame, nature and beauty and of course power and prestige. It is also a reflection of how being a youth comes with a lot of responsibility rather than being a nut-case who is on a buoyant trip to nowhere.

I hope that these poems will encourage and inspire readers in a positive and purpose driven way. I also hope that this book will be a resting place in the ear of your heart and a portal for the eyes to your mind.

Vagi Samuel Jnr.
June, 2018

Vagi Samuel Jnr.

CONTENTS

Vagi Samuel Jnr.

SENIS BILONG YUMI WER? (TOK PISIN)

Tok-tok bilong man lo sens ino nau nau
Gutpela save man pepa blo yu wokim wanem wok?
Senis bilong pikinini e stap long skul
Bilong wanem emi e raun natin lo stap?
Senis bilong susa e stap long haus
Banis bilong paol raun yu pasim doa tu o?
Senis bilong barata e stap long bik bus na solwara
Pasin bilong tumbuna taim diriman lo wer stap?
Senis bilong papa e stap long wok-moni
Het bilong pik painim wanem long bia garden?
Senis bilong mama e stap long haus lotu
Hevi bilong tok-baksait yu tanim tok lo wanem samtin?
Senis bilong bubu-man e stap long haus man
Bilong wanem em e selim kalapua na wokim bilak pawa?
Senis bilong bubu-meri e stap long haus kuk
Bilong wanem em e palai antap olosem bilak bokis?
Senis bilong peles e stap long ol man na meri
Bunara na busnaip painin birua long wanem samtin?
Senis bilong komuniti e stap long wod-kaunsel
Kauboi kep na niuspepa painim wanem wok wantaim
Lidaman?
Senis bilong kauntri e stap long pipol
Gavaman bilong wanem yu planim giaman tin-tin?
Senis bilong gavaman e stap long praim minista
Pasin bilong honest wok rausim em sea kin blo em
Pinis bilong giraun e kam klostu nau
Bai yumi wokim wanem tete?
Na tu senis bilong yumi olgeta e stap wer?
Askim ol arapela lain wer oli no stap ples klia
Na senis bilong yu wer?
Askim lo level bilong ol man blo blok
Na senis bilong mi wer?
Mi askim pinis lo namba tu lain blo disla tok sing sing yah!

For I Too Am a Papua New Guinean

I am forty
I am a Christian
I am beautiful
And I am the land of the unexpected.

From the crawling of the dawn
Alotau gives birth to the sun as it raises discreetly humming
"Eh, that one how"
Humble winds from Oro sends morning greetings on
The wings of Queen Alexandria butterfly
That, its sound almost wakes Fly River
To begin the day by strumming its subtle streams
And as Kerema sings a vocal rendition in adoring its line
'Yu yet kam na lukim'
Your highness, Hiri Queen sways her hips from
The lagatoi in a harmonic pattern with the waves
Perhaps, once more Captain Moresby
Is incarnated into this transitional day
Are you from Southern Region, Maybe?
For I too, am a Papua New Guinean.

As morning divorces the noon
Raging seas from Bismarck quests onto the atolls
Of copper-less Bougainville
The white sandy beaches and dives signal
A beautiful lady called New Ireland
Courtesy deeds from Kimbe through
All natives is dubbed as 'Pasin West'
More often, smoke from notorious Tavurvur
In the East has doomed humanity
For this reason apart, foreign refugees
Have also found comfort in nearby Lorengau
Are you from the Islands Region, Maybe?
For I too, am a Papua New Guinean.

By the time a dog barks
A tribal fight welcomes Tari with open arms
And swinging tramontina bush knifes
It pushes further up and restrains as Wapenamanda
Ends the dog from its barking
From valleys of mist squall an incense of flora
from the mighty muruk garas
Up the rugged terrain of a tranquil backdrop
Plies lime-stones of Simbu
Through orange quarry and thick breeze
Is the seldom scene of Mount Hagen
Before the hunters of Jiwaka repatriate
For a huge feast for abstaining from clashes
Peaceful mud man from Asaro
Burn their spears as the afternoon cold covers highlands
Are you from the Highlands Region, Maybe?
For I too, am a Papua New Guinean.

As the evening reckons a rest,
Voices etched in the shivers from Apo land
Releases serenity to the beautiful Flying Fox City
Wopa Country delights in the aftermath of the journey
That began 40 years on September 16, 1975
The man behind it all, Sir Michael Thomas Somare
Who hails from the East rivers of crocodiles
To our destiny for another 40, a wish for God's favor
As the sun sets once more in Sandaun province
Are you from Momase Region, Maybe?
For I too, am a Papua New Guinean.

Vagi Samuel Jnr.

PNG: OLD ENOUGH TO BE ANYTHING

I stand amidst a period of economic growth
And a sense of hypocrisy
But I feast from Aus. Aid and yet I still thrust to steal
I labour the resources from the land and drink from the sea
But I devour the owner's dues and yet whine I do not heal.

What is your name? Papua New Guinea
And do you have a surname? Yes. Christian Country
How old are you now? Old enough, I'm forty
Where do you come from? The pacific ring of fire.

Sons and daughters quest on from sports and politics
National and Post gossip about me back to front
I wear the red, black and gold but never in black and white
Does Sunday ring a bell in your ear?

Why, is that your pride reaches mount Wilhelm?
Have you ever heard of O arise, reporter?
I shout again for the whole world to hear
Why? Coz white men and *kon-kon* give me kina and toea.

THE MASK OF INDEPENDENCE

Masquerade or desperate!
I wear a smile on my face to fend of animosity
Yet my pride neither defends hate nor positivity
I wear curiosity on my face
To know answers for many questions
Yet I complain for reasons unknown
With too many suggestions
I wear thumbs up on my face
To tell out the good works of government
Yet my inner most being repels the core of deeds they bend
I wear rage on my face to transfer desolations of hell
Yet I denounce peace in isolation for segregation to sell
I wear humility on my face to flush out my weakness
Yet my growth for righteousness is diminished by wickedness
I wear the red-black-gold on my face to hail unity
Yet I stand amongst tribes of thousand men to teach mutiny
I wear black and white on a Sunday morning
Yet I swear vulgar and repeat cries from a hut
For the reason of mourning
I wear a shadow of doubt every single day
Is this life a masquerade or desperate? I wouldn't say!

JUST THE OTHER DAY

I saw a man in torn clothes
Sitting in the scorching heat
A cupboard placed at a street
His palms open
Did you spare a coin or some notes?

I saw a woman consoling her children
Walking on a wet footpath
Braving the cold and the dirt
Yet her smile so golden
Did you offer her a helping hand?

I saw a convoy of young boys
Each carrying a sack of plastic bottles
Taking cover at the splash of pot-holes
The driver's sins forgotten
Would you stop to buy them some toys?

I saw a group of school girls
Chewing *buai* and smoking cigarettes
A few man crossed the line and made duets
Yet their future is begotten
Would you stop them from having turns?

I saw a doctor at the emergency
Watching movies and playing games
A sick child at the door crying like flames
Wrapped up in cotton
Do you even have some decency?

I saw a waiter at an expatriate shop
Serving the white man so humble and agile
Snubbing the local customer by the aisle
Fueled with embarrassment
Is that how the floor is mopped?

I saw a kid today
Playing with a dog at his backyard
Parents at the core of his reward
Then, I thought to myself
Why didn't I see this the other day?

I am Innocent

I stand with a trembling body
A harsh anger thought crippled by fear
Fear in a sense where desperation of a life
I so deserve as a child being deprived hidden
My right to freedom is shattered and forgone
Mother scold's me like a stray dog nomadic
Foul language being her slang of choice
The feeling is like I am not welcomed at all
Rejection and corporal punishment reintroduced
Father fists me like a boxing bag swaying all direction
He legs me like a soccer ball bulleting like a strikers pick
I gasped for air but then he takes pride simultaneously
I utter my utmost beseech for my fair say of innocence
However, their ever raging presence is felt by me
Crushed by hopelessness, emptied being helpless
Disgrace to my friends I am completely worthless
I kneel on my knees with sheer quiver and shiver
Now, speechless with a disfigured face and bruised body
Almost at the verge of bleeding to my destiny
I lay low unconscious with nothing to lose but
With dignity and honor to the stature of a child
I am innocent.

THE DARKER VERSION

I am not the enemy
I am the result of your excuses
You are not my nemesis
You are girly-girly.

I am not a book cover
I am the bank of expression
You are the depression
You seek to uncover.

I am not the words you read
I am the truth you hear by page
You are the hate
You find in yourself so unreal.

I am not the white man
I am the darker version
You are the immersion
You boast in your fine linen.

I am not the pain
I am the vessel of change
You are the negate
You belittle what I paint.

I am not old school
I am the latest software
You are the hardware
You walk and act like we cool.

We are not the same
We are what PNG needs to see
They struggle, strive and plea
They are after all, our mate!

FREEDOM!

Hope;
want of the extraordinary
unorthodox pleasures
need to achieve in life
drowning from knowing.

Desire;
errands of longing
suffering internally
bubbles of indulgence
as self-worth diminishes.

Love;
the lynching of a soul
where gestures of the old mind
reserves the unrighteous
defeat – animosity grins.

Choices;
array of yearnings on call
fifty thousand thoughts of fusion
data mining line by line
ready to be consecrated.

Decision;
separated power to produce
knowledge at the sight of reverie
from wisdom are battles won
one voice doomed by many questions.

Commitment;
where paths of speech act
the reaction to every action
mind to hand and heart to feet
lead on where destiny awaits.

Fear;
teasing courage off guard
pause without boundaries
leaves faith hanging
on walls of darkened calamity.

Freedom;
the right to breath amongst men
achingly desperate forms
of peace serving anarchy
and where order feeds on security.

Humor;
the sound of happiness
sensationalism!
quenching pain with ecstasy
pulchritude – every bit of glee.

Home;
where identity calls me by name
blood becomes the portal
permeating values and customs
renaissance - a hand shake with freedom.

DECENT PENNY

Penny plays on the back of decency
Put on a smile that needy child deserves
He just might bury all 'em sad reserves
As you heel up the journey without complacency.

Many of those begging strangers grin to ply
Within their hearts beam a light of hope
Wedged amongst strife is their glorious throne
But we abled brethren always devour to imply.

Saints from our memories sting us to recall
Claps of praise shall we invite to honor
But of thriving men concede partners of donor
To man of hate thy thumb shall indulge in a fall.

So spare them a bob will you?
Not that notes own your whole being, does it?
Or rather an ounce of love to share seem just a few
Keep giving as this world is governed by power and profit.

UNEARTH SOLITUDE

Haste with this solemn inquiry, will you?
For time shall detour progress thus far
Factors beyond our reach are close by
And may delve into unyielding scars.

Lest we forget the notions of impetus
For corruption that ungrateful man might
Dice on the banquet of noble status
Will this be another disgusting fight?

Gestures we seek to unearth are covered
By those who call themselves honest
Yet all that belongs to men are governed
By those whom we should call dishonest.

For the righteous that delivers silently
May his work flourish without statements
For the unrighteous that gives publicly
His left-hand shall own self entitlements.

What they may have done at all
To all peoples it's another dream
Where peoples may have not seen at all
To them it's another solitude realm.

VICTORY AT THE TOP

Mountains of life I climb
Are mounts of pressure that bind
Rocks I step on with faith
Let go negative slides of pain.

Moments I have a rest
The further is Mount Everest
Minutes of those who pass me by
I have no proof of my alibi.

The climbers before me progress
I succumb to issues of regress
Thirst of winning and hunger for success
I keep toiling on to the top of my prowess.

I am weeping and howling, but am steadfast
Because the ascending is risky and rough
Hands shaking to grip with all my body part
Victory! Shouted I, for I have beaten all that was tough.

AGENTS OF CHANGE

My state of consciousness is abruptly shaken
Thoughts deterred and emotions shattered
Hypnotized by unusual and strange confrontation
By right, must I be granted courage to deliver outrage?

Unseen things of the future still imaged pitch black
Taste of dreams capture nothing but empty hopes
Instincts surprise the present and threatens self-thought
By right, must I be granted wisdom to detonate negation?

Complacency and procrastination steal progress
Ill-management of time fuel and burn laziness
The way forward is hindered by unplanned commotion
By right, must I be granted leverage to challenge status quo?

My beliefs remain focused and composed
Behavior tolerant but optimistically motivated
Attitudes rise and liberty prevails in the clutters
By right, must I be granted freedom to cure differences?

UNI-TECH RALLY FOR JUSTICE!

One man challenged the status quo
Dared by certainty to dethrone corruption
As he pleaded never fear the duo
Lead me onward for knowledge restitution.

Where brilliant minds congregate
Notions of prosperity amalgamate
When they all speaketh
Humanity indulges in their might from hereon.

Voice the truth you devious man
Conspiring fails integrity
Kiss the issue dear woman
Bleach your dealings with positivity.

We look ahead
We toil on this righteous path
Sooner is the day of our redemption
Where we shall dine with victory and justice.

We stand – No Schram, No School.

CHASED

Beneath the sole of thy feet
Remain scars that tread paths unimaginable
Tattered and yet hastes to shine past defeat
To whom shall tis vanity be conceivable?

Through words of disgust, another dare
From zero tags to questioning of birth right
Engraved within thee is a soul so bare
That of which degenerates breathe for life.

Sirens from the law envies my receptive ears
A glimpse of revolving red and blue lights trace
Heels that stride like black deeds for many years
Prison waits in vain as I have vanished in this race.

An afternoon's walk in the street of late residence
Kids playing hopscotch while boys behooving on rolls
A dog enters the scene galloping with resurgence
I foot the white line defiant to blood with no more strolls.

Then, I tremble for anxiety has pierced my world
For the taste of violence has denied my existence
Another gunpoint from afar offer no resistance
Rather wounds from pets, have I now to front the end?

I am my run chase
The denigrate of my soul
I am my dark phase
After all, the enemy of my own.

Beneath the sole of thy feet
Remain scars that tread paths unimaginable
Tattered and yet hastes to shine past defeat
To whom shall tis vanity be conceivable?

DIVIDING LINES

From golden rays that haze atop the sea
Spits from the ocean carry a wonderful sound
Like the conch shell that ripples its voice
Far stretched out beyond the horizon
Deep like the famous Marianna trench
I am captivated.

I see beauty that slowly drains my burdens
Shouldered by my thoughts and soul
But I cannot count them in this silhouette
For they are like the waves that crawl onto the beach
Dressed in white crisps covered in black silk
I am cornered.

I release my stress in the evening wind
That is bound by guilt and shame
My heart beats in the aftermath
And I hear the beseeches and screams
Not far from the war memorial cemetery
I am tested.

I feel the fire beneath my two feet
The cry of darkness that meets by flesh
An impending reaction at a cross road
The image of a black stained casket;
And a burning light on a narrow footpath
I am battered.

Suddenly, I pray to master;
For you I shall decrease
And through me you shall increase
I beg you to replenish my soul
And cleanse my weeping spirit
I am truly purified.

A SIMPLE VILLAGER (HANUA TAUNA)
(A poem in English and Motu)

There was a time
in this life
that I remember
what I was taught.

to mend the reke
to empty the tua
and paddle the vanagi
for another hoada.

There was a time
in this life
that I remember
what I was taught.

to sharpen the ilapa
to weave the gagama
and walk the taora
for another raka.

There was a time
in this life
that I remember
what I was taught.

to oil the ira
to gather the puses
and skipper the hagwa
for another au-abi.

There was a time
in this life
that I remember
what I was taught.

to fix the vada
to gather the rau
and wrap the biku
for another gumi-gumi.

There was a time
in this life
that I remember
what I was taught.

to sleep at hanuaboi
to watch my taiagu
and wake at first diari
for another daba-ahu.

There was a time
in this life
that I remember
what I was taught.

to sort out the toboca
to fill up the kiapa
and track the tarua
for another hado-hado.

There was a time
in this life
that I remember
what I was taught.

to wait for the davara
to let it become komada
and carry the karaudi
for another rago-rago.

There was a time
in this life

that I remember
what I was taught.

to wipe the ipidi
to clean the kasilesi
and lurk from the nese
for another labana.

There was a time
in this life
that I remember
what I was taught.

to remember the hanua maurina
to do all these sene gaukaradia
and be called a tau and hane lohia
for the life today and tomorrow!

DIMINISHING CREATION

Rough and smooth waves evade the shores
Submerged foot prints engrave the sandy beach
The once pure and clean coastline
Have become a bed for disposable waste on the frontline.

Trees and high shrubs canopy the mass land
Savannah across disguising drier patches and bushes
The once vast dancing and swaying green fields
Have become an eye saw of rubbish dump, landfills.

Birds and insects hover and rule over the blue sky
Maneuvering clouds decorate and shade the land and sea
The once imperative layers and cosmic spheres
Have become a labor ward for emitted foreign gaseous.

Natural beauty and glamour are gradually diminishing
As man-made developments vanquish thy creation
Flora and fauna are our foremost priority to care take
Lest we forget the rarity of destitution will take effect.

OUR MISSION IN LIFE

Life is happiness as others say it is so mean
It drowns us with seas of problem dynamites
That kills trees of man like wood-eating termites
Lead by its ruler; the notorious and glorious queen.

It stamps its mark as truthful and real
Conquering every captive dreams we have had
Regardless of any other distinct or equal deal
Whether we perceive as indeed good or bad.

We can merely be fond of its aspects
Or be tested by its provisions and necessities
But if we cannot cope with its prospects
We will never vanquish all its basic properties.

Our mission is life is not to be without problem or pain
But a continual habit to sustain fluent gains
Whether the moments of time that defines us
Life is destined to be indispensable without a fuss.

SENEMAI TRADITION

I am amazed with the splendid display
Of traditional attire and synchronized maneuver
An array of tuned beats and pattern creation
Complimented by a grooving sensation.

It's a seldom scene virgin by ancient right
Moved by this piece of historical re-enactment
I am almost at the brink of drowning myself
In the pools of customs and cultural insights.

What else more can I reminisce about?
When I am fed with the meander of ritualistic era!
I would rather envelope myself
In this mind captivating journey
Then just ware away in a looming nervous break-down.

It's a rewarding depiction of valuing my true identity
Sacramental to the normal way of life
I feel a sense of belonging because that's my roots
Founded upon beliefs and values in Senemai traditions.

THE LIFE WITHIN

Life begins with someone
Relates to another being
It challenges everyone
But gives eternal living.

It can be a complicated journey
With remorse and agitated manners
The tranquil of its beauty exists
But it can only be if we relive.

People view it as a mere drama
A thin fabric that covers its trauma
Others believe in its offers
But are countered by its norm losers.

Its sophisticated nature replenishes emptiness
Surrounded by inevitable dilemmas
As we ought to live simplicity
But that life is within without strife.

MY HOME

O how sad is my home?
Parted it when I was still young
She needs my hand to work
For she envies my helping potential.

O how beautiful is her shore line?
Smiling at ocean liners with different colors
Free from us all but attached forever
Holding present and past times with dignity.

O how strong is her charisma?
The cold wind swaying her coconut trees
Raging storms basking her innocence
As she stands firm with an energetic foundation.

O how faithful is her culture?
Living a life with a feast of treasure
Bathing with the water of values
With a splendid array of norms and traditions.

AN HONOR

The wisdom of the old-age produces substance of truth
Their uttered words remain with the legacy of great harvest
Their characters display flawless integrity, authentic
The legend of the great Vagi Rage I pay homage too.

Those who are of righteousness bless their bloodline
Off those who walk with sinister curse with longevity
People who inherit the blessing possess noble qualities
As those who are blight accede to the world's satisfaction.

I am honored to be called like the great
As it gives me a sense of ownership and responsibility
The blessings of my grandfather sowed into the future
A destiny optimistic cemented by opportunity and time.

Pride consumes me as I have found my place to be
My people approve of my dignity and stature
They need my hands and head for its no predicament
But a foretaste of what that is inside of me.

THE LONE RISK TAKER

I am alone
Yet I'm unlimited
I see nothing
But I feel them all.

Freedom is mine
Yet I am secluded
I am engraved
But before me is plain.

Am I scared?
Maybe
Am I weak?
Could be.

Being free isn't all
For I don't care
I am
The risk taker.

MATCHLESS

I have credentials that qualify me above you
I have standards to maintain then to level you palm-off
I have integrity to withstand you stuck-up from denying me
I have principles unmatched by you looser
I set the Bars; you haven't and will not even reach
I am
Matchless.

A DAY'S BIRTH

The cold of mourning
Huddled the village
Must its crest bug?
Not even until pests rise.

Then, shall gloom commune
Under soothing quests
Where dew amasses
All slide into a dull day.

Have its rings glare
In distant pardon
Lurking amongst thorns
Are waiting gills of hope.

Before the day's end
The fading sun quivers
For the peak of evening
Another night defends dawn.

HUMANITY RISES

The lust of pride is endless
Cues that cultivate destitute
Are searing onward further
Fathoming are 'I did' chants.

Beyond the horizon of frail
Desolation arrests oscillation
Where boasting tears fail
But to no avail shall I gain.

Mercy has chained tis zeal
Greater the pain resonate
To whom shall freedom sail
As self-worth plies to detonate.

A soul's right to breathe
Is where freedom really exists
If he shall not fend for his fate
Then only shall he toil in faith.

Setbacks paint walls of hope
The fall of men is evident
Where all hell gears down
Humility shall make you great.

SELFLESSNESS

I am aggravated
It comes from anger
Anxiety is apparent but isn't that what experience is?
Selfishness too is attached to these glaring perceptions
Either mentally or emotionally
Why deprive myself from happiness
For something unproductive?
It doesn't pay huge dividends to life itself
Am I a coward? Maybe
But all the above are certainties in life
Norms are evident and I just hope
That glee supersedes my whole.
I succumb to selflessness in search of liberty.

SURPRISED

Neither am I
Further haste you shall
Quiver received along the hall
Gather all that meets your eye.

I AM ME

Beat your chest before weak men
You that hides within layers of secrecy
Be that taste of classic fallacy
Drink to the banalities of death my friend.

Disguise your lips with phrases of praise
I am and I did quotes are far more rhetoric
Atonement to words unheard of like a maze
As always your ways are empty to nothing historic.

RID OF PRIDE

Hallow these winds of karma
Blow them pride driven punks
Your swirling rage punch them
Must they fall within average life.

Change bring 'em onto their knees
Teach them with humble deeds
Let their innate beam like glory
To uncharted waters may they sail.

Smoothing wonders of peace wave
Unto their demise must you rise
Mend the pores from bleeding sins
Heal once more their wrecked souls.

Farewell the winds of karma
Leave those who have been taught
I beseech your presence again
When pride ashore home once more!

PEACE AT ELA BEACH

The smell of the sand raced at me
The sea gently raping the beach
West pulled by view to the hill of trees
As perfect meditation suited within reach.

Spare me a dose of the setting sun
So that this picture is framed in my heart
Post me a comment as pleasing as fun
#Tag; I was dreaming before it got dark.

Let this moment play like an iTunes hit
A sound that is blown from a conch shell
May this evening resemble a mending kit
As Ela Beach draws me to home's return.

THE STORY BEHIND

The story of the past
Makes me think so east
As slow as it can last
Life seems like an out-cast
In its dream as it must
I slowly begin to rust.

Vagi Samuel Jnr.

The Late Line

The night so cold
With the wind very bold
And as the music began to unfold
The moon was semi-bright as gold.

Forming through the sky were clouds
That happened to be a nice groove
So light, free, gentle were the sounds
As comfort with perfect harmony did grew.

Dark places sparkled with delight
Every shadow portraying dull figures
With glowing stars with perfect light
Just like bullet sparks missing ducking diggers.

Echoing were undefined voices of the wild
With strange lurking creatures lurking align
Impending reactions very young and mild
As I slowly got lost in forgone in line.

A MAN

From the Hands of God, he was made
From his rib, a woman came into being
From him and a she, a family is created
Who is he? A man.

A man was given dominion
and authority over all things
His roles are to provide care, security
protection and guidance
A man to us is a leader by example to
our home and to our community
With wisdom, knowledge and understanding
bestowed upon him.

What is a man?

He is a brother to his younger and older siblings
He is an uncle to nieces and nephews
He is a *bubu-man* to his grand-children
But most of all
A husband to his wife and a father to his children

A father stands tall and upright
His pride is his work and his family
He is not defined by muscles or his standing
But he is defined by 'God to be the head of the house'
To love his wife and discipline his children
With Christian principles.

So, let this day, be a day of purpose, honor
Praise and thanks-giving!

SPARING CONVERSATIONS

Tell me a joke that I may not laugh
I may not glee at all but to its spell I will jest
But even if I did show my Colgate teeth
Does that encapsulate a chuckle?

Let me chuckle to the nothingness of your utterance
You can devour me to the thrust of evil
If a bad constitutes a humor in disguise
Will that be a subject of good or bad?

You can create a bad impression on me
Get all the loose ends and hail your beauty
But if I am that ugly and you are a princess
Will that make me a Shrek or a jerk?

Define jerk?
A looser without a handsome face!
What is a princess then?
A loner without the rescue of a jerk.

DYING MAN

Life didn't admit the gasp of his age
Painful chest wounded by a mucus wall
Perhaps fathoming on debris of triage
That we are jailed by clichés after all.

Demand comes the hour of a window
That light and air seem so near to us
Pardons the meaning of our truce
As destitution avenges forth a shadow.

Flashbacks draw sketches of his destiny
Beyond imaginations that vaguely pry
Deeds reverse entry to derail longevity
As ghosts of the end crawl in to ply.

Seconds of humaneness suck him out
Neither shall tis essence of hope shine
Merely are his eyes painting tears about
Death, for us all he leaves us behind!

THE GREAT FALL

The silence of my mind
Has kept me at bay
Thoughtless is this computer
Like still shots motionless
What am I to do?
SPEAK.
Delusional sentiments
Are free from sanity
Have you lost your mind?
TALK.
Palm cards escape my hands
As they spray beside my feet
Aren't you gonn' do something?
MOVE.
The steaming eyes of students
Robbing me of from self-esteem
Well, retreat to your seat then?
Instantly, a complete shutdown
No prompt! No pop-up icon!
Onto the floor is my trembling body
My entirety vibrating like a ringtone
I have just fallen on my debate final
AMBULANCE.

TIS PRAYER I PRAY

Shake off the dust from gloomy yesterday
Glorious waters of grace awaits my bath
Mercy shall put on me a fresh garment then
Knitted in love like the blue sky I see today.

Have me the food that my heart delights in
Fruits from the Gospel that feeds my spirit
Defend the sagging walls within my mind
So my soul shall be guarded from evils trick.

Not alone shall I thread in absent places
Mountains that steal light from dark valleys
Be it the stormy rains serving drought plains
The great giver of life shall my mouth please.

Let me meet him who renews me everyday
An encounter beyond life come what may
He listens to all my pleas that my tears play
Tis prayer I pay to invest in another new day.

YET I STAND SEARCHING

From sharing is man selfless
Have you heard of love?
From smiling is man happy
Have you heard of joy?
From silence is man wiser
Have you heard of peace?
From contention is man steadfast
Have you heard of patience?
From giving is man hearted
Have you heard of kindness?
From sin is man forgiven
Have you heard of goodness?
From darkness is man lightened
Have you heard of faithfulness?
From timidity is man lifted
Have you heard of gentleness?
From temptation is man secured
Have you heard of self-control?

BENEATH THE OLD RAIN TREE

Beneath the old rain tree I wondered
About how this good friend of mine
Standing with its sleeveless branches
Wrinkled skin peeling off from its body
But still smiling to offer a free service
And yet – mankind has been ignorant
I wondered.

It didn't rain for days
But it stood there braving the sun
It was thirsty for water
But it only gained from the heat.

The sun didn't shine no more
But it stood there braving the cold
It was shivering for warmth
But it only lost weight at night.

It didn't share its pain
But it stood there braving the wind
It danced in the moonlight stars
But it only shrank in the morning.

It didn't cry out loud
But it stood there braving the cuts
It turned red in a fire place
But it never grew after being amputated.

It didn't warn many kids
But it stood there laughing at them
It became skinless at school
But it was known to be a teacher's pride.

It didn't complain about the ride
But it stood there taking a punch.

It became a commodity
But it was sacrificed after depreciation.

It didn't say a word to RH
But it stood there watching them decapitate
It became barren to mother-nature
But it still shines even after being buried.

Beneath the old rain tree I wondered
About how it stood there – freely
Sheltering me from the heat
Dancing with the wind
Offering a grin at the sun
Even after I left – it just stood there waving its leaves!

STINTS FROM RAINY LAE

A million drops to its peoples
Its people call it blessing
Blessings to the urban villages
To the sailing canoes from Labu Butu
The rugged cliffs of Buang
Down the plains of Leron
Passionate to winds from Salamaua
Cloudy to Finschaffen
Pleasure to the clays of Menyama!
It's called rain washing all Morobeans!
Home, were the heart grows fonder.

THE INK MASTER

Amongst fading thoughts that will never cease to exist
Resonate, a thousand words that my mouth longs to speak
Buried deep within my mind that resists to be weak
Abundance of reasoning lust for my thirsty hands to frisk.

Wild is this journey that begins with an empty page
Each line that is ruled for an alphabetical marathon or
A stanza that send words to preach about this race
Offer gifts of unheard voices to come to the fore.

For every ink that drops onto a blank space, echo a whistle
Not that it blows about to arrest big minds so little
Nor does it alarm to withdraw transitioning silence
But to perform surgery to so many deaf ears.

Free verse is the playground of traversing conversations
Lingering in the moments where thinking is stalled
Dictionary brushing away dirt from itching sensations
For the sake of knowing, another reader is called.

Perhaps time is at the brink of extinction, to be free
Straight, mental menstruation on a democratic spree
Emotions that run through veins of clarity cheer on
For the finish line has ransomed me from hereon.

From the peak of mount Wilhelm transcend this creed
Even from the left wings to the right, twist and glide
I am that instrument rejoicing from the depths of my feet
An expression that lifts gently for freedom is forever mine.

To a writer, shall his mind be sober to a drunken nation
His pen making love to barren streets of literacy gates
Every creative line shall bear fruits of truth and restoration
Reaching desperate souls where another ink master awaits.

TRANCE

In a distant glory is he's strength
Shoulders soar with arms so square
An evil smile that rents on a barren face
Loan me a chance is an un-registered voice.

Then, there she stands amongst pity men
Looking all so precious priced like diamond rings
Only to note she's queued up to grab her drink
On the rocks as she hangs on a line to tease them

He sweeps in with quotes from an old movie
Madam! Can I buy you a drink?
She breaks the trend with a gullible burst
Dude? You are just a kid, go read a book.

He pauses for seconds before smothering the space
If I told you that I liked you then I would be lying
She pledges "so what would a guy like you say?"
Dudette? Seriously, get the fuck out of my face!

DAY DREAMER

The coconut tree curtained by back
As the mesmerizing view planed the deck
I watched the sun fade into the ocean
As the crashing waves blazed into motion
Before the crickets could turn to singing
A lonesome feeling bathed me with gazing
I groped the platform to induce freelance
But the cool breeze harassed my innocence
Often at times, anxiety begging more space
But the demise ventured without a debate
Then, a thought to fend off alienation came
But the unusual ordinary grew stale
Suddenly, at once it dawned on me
And before I could speak as I ought to be
The only place that I had ever dreamt off
Quickly, re-gathered my thoughts thereof
That, if this wasn't the foreground of reality
Nor the burst of my dreams into eternity
I realized then that the embalming nature
Of day-dreaming about the unknown future
Has not just paid me an elicit
But a nomadic visit!

HIS UNIVERSE

As God spoke
The universe formed
His hands touched
And man was born.

The sky ogled the land
Lightning basking the thunder
As the day is envious of his night
Her moon smiles at the eclipse of the solar.

The clouds of heaven crying
Tears of joy for all the earth
As the wind blows onto her skin
Splendid the waves come calling me.

All things came into being!

MIRACULOUS MADANG TRIP

Towards the sleeves of Leron
Miracle rode her body along
Passengers' on-board singing sail on
As the journey to Madang seemed short.

Roadside stalls one to many
A booming grassroots business
One-stop customers there upon plenty
A relieving sensation ripping stress.

Gusty winds spray our progress
Dust painting our faces at the rear
Driver wearing the speed dress
As Ramu Valley filmed nearer.

Usino bathed us in a glorious rain
Detour ahead by a felled tree blockade
A Rambo banking on fee-ed passage
As coins cycled into his pocket drain.

Tapo greeted us with a trenched river
Check-point didn't issue our traverse
Bitumen framed us a soothing shiver
As Madang glided us in Miracle's Canvas.

PRAISE THE LORD

Memories of the past
Arguing with the present
The still moments cast
Spells of all that is absent.

I search the horizon everyday
Hoping to claim what is lost
I come every Friday
And feel the presence of our host.

People, young and old smile
The single expression of life
Some heed the call to strive
Yet we all give meaning to life.

Conscious of our programs
Everyone share and laugh
The environment is like diagrams
Of love images without bluff.

Laziness is not a language
Participation and cooperation glow
Diversity resembling our luggage
All become one ready just to plough.

A grin on my face tells of happiness
Mirrored by another to be lifted
We all harvest goodness
But we are all by right gifted.

I write with all that I am
Lines of emotions and feelings
Undiscovered God given talents
Are now paramount tonight.

Let us sing and dance
Let us raise our voices and hands
With three big claps and say
Halleluiah, praise the lord.

RETURN TO THE MAKER

Sing a song you that are worried
Let not your mind rape you apart
But immerse in the lyrical path
So all your wastes can be buried.

Read a bible verse you angry man
Tis phase requires silent meditation
Serenity is only found in restoration
Just release so peace you shall earn.

Smile a while you that is saddened
Receive all wounds with happiness
Heal your thorns without bitterness
As your inner value gets whitened.

You all man who are living astray
Return to the lord with confession
Seek the grace of God within to stay
Welcome love with self-satisfaction.

Vagi Samuel Jnr.

SESTINA: WE WERE NEVER A MATCH!

We were never a match
She was a crusader from birth
I was a realist during high school years
We had different ideas and opinions
From the time we started to date
We both pursued dreams not the same.

Everything was just the same
Black and white could never match
But December twenty-fifth was the date
That our friendship gave birth
I did not hate but her opinions
For I cared so much for the coming years.

Beautiful was the last three years
Maybe for love we became the same
We debated and agreed on our opinions
We held hands in public like we were a match
We cried as rugged as babies at birth
For we called every secluded meeting a date.

But then I forgot our anniversary date
And rage consumed her all through the years
From the night's death to the dawns birth
We never kissed for the sun did not shine the same
We were lovers in disguise at the strike of a match
Renting on the flames stolen by her darkened opinions.

We talked – nothing changed but still her opinions
Grew stale like the moon on a thunderous date
What could have I done to make us a match?
For destiny's sake, would there still be us years?
Rain came on different days; the storm was still the same
Definite was the thought, could our end be at birth?

Then, I gnawed my teeth and remembered my date of birth
That I have been twirled into oblivion by fruitless opinions
For this love story was history, records not the same
For every yesterday was a stagnant date
Like time drinking away my blood, depreciating the years
At the cost of love; could we still be a match?

For if we ain't a match, will the evil inside you give birth
To blessed years without
The production of constipated opinions?
If so, how does a romantic date sound
At the expense of us being the same?

TERZA RIMA: DOMESTIC LOVE

There you see her with all her best
You feed on her like a succulent plant
While she's full you are never a beast.

Then, you praise her and spend
Money on silver and gold laces just a few
In order to keep up with the city trend.

Then, you make her feel like she's brand new
You crack jokes, laugh as she giggles
Making her think of course you are true.

Then, there comes a time with no more jingles
She seems all is well and rebuts your say
Next minute – the flame fades in the hustles.

There she stands by the door to run away
Leaving the moon not to glow anymore in the dark
She wonders if the sun can quickly give birth to day

Lest, the nights' get longer when the dogs' bark
Even the cats' too, could hear her scream, mother!
You put blood on her blouse at the public park.

She admits at the emergency with her father
Forever, you disappear at the sight of her big brother.

VILLANELLE: LIFE AND MARRIAGE

In his arms she slept quietly, all through the night
For love had struck her eyes beyond infinity
Wedding, she said gladly with sheer delight.

Who would have thought if she was Ms. Right?
Thoughts engraved his heart with her beauty
In his arms she slept quietly, all through the night.

She was sexy but dressed by her fathers might
How she made him laugh and gave him a duty
Wedding, she said gladly with sheer delight.

For every kiss meant that they wouldn't fight
A hug sent shivers cascading down her body
In his arms she slept quietly, all through the night.

Even in times of weakness and strife
Love did not weaver nor did they feel guilty
Wedding, she said gladly with sheer delight.

How often do we evaluate our life?
For all we can do for now is picture the story
In his arms she slept quietly, all through the night
Wedding, she said gladly with sheer delight.

GREEN GOLD OF GOROKA

Hessian bags of green gold
strung up in layers like pillows
there stood a man by the willows
wondering how his beans will be sold.

I passed by Korofegu station
as showers of the morning plead
for the humble sun to be free
from the thick mist from the plantation.

I fetched the pain in his eyes
his beard masking selflessness
and in that moment of stillness
my heart visited all his cries.

I wondered how he'd appeal
eloping with the dawn's cold
at an hour that seemed so old
yet fresh but truly surreal.

I whispered a prayer of solace
amidst the calamity of this nation
from urban villages to this outstation
imparting heaven's gift to embrace.

I buried the scenic aroma
in the lips of my dried mind
sipping on the finest grind
of coffee from *kolples* Goroka.

SHADOWS

Like the stars above
I plea at the sky
On my knees to shove
All my sins and try
To slain doubt
And defeat the world
Leave no traces about
The past to claim my health.

TAMAGU EH! (OH MY FATHER!)

He is the man I call dad
The man of coke
He smells like Fanta orange
Or perhaps like pineapple
After work just like the factory
I am grateful paps!
I guess we have been living
On the coke side of life.

SONNET 1: HELAOREA (STRIFE)

The rivulet of nega
Grins on the chest of hora
As her spells devour raka
Keto melodies onward to moru
Uma has plead for mercy
Thieves beckoning after dark
What little Hanua has sown?
Henao plays his story along
What more can Mauri do?
Manoka has sent for goada
But the odds still favour dohore
Gabeai produces metau
As Maduna shoulders hisi-hisi
Where the hell is hahodi then?

SONNET 2: IN MEMORY OF THE FUTURE

The future is fore
Ahead from my present
The past is all that's gone
Laid to rest in the absent
What is today then?
The spring of infinity
Now, begins my destiny
When tomorrow walks with thee
Then shall thy start with the end
For all that thy ought to bend
Need not the worst of thee
And that thy sense of glee
Shall glance at a thriving future
Not with the wrath of mother nature.

SONNET 3: MY LAE CITY

Heat of this place I call home
Rest assured its might be known
Tantalizing shaft of pigment own
Nothing more than sunburnt alone
Cold of its lustful nature tend more
Dull shall power the heavens lift
Descend tiny drops into water galore
Called rain toward humanities gift
An era of development face its path
Vanishing potholes cum cement seal
A Nadzab highway to be in line of quad
The extended basin for its port zeal
Surely shall this place be not that dirty
Even when you visit my Lae city.

SONNET 4: LOVE I SEE NOW

Love I see now is etched on flesh
The kind that ink is tattooed on skin
One feels the pain during its making
Blood is a ransom for this experience
Then, comes the rubbing of body oil
A perfectionist's will to pay marvel
Time shall heal this pardon of stain
Only when attention is pursued well
Behold of its beauty now it portrays
Perform this game of vulnerability
Harm is within reach of squander
Like pulse that engage on thin veins
That clings with uncertainty everyday
But does that encapsulate true love?

SONNET 5: I WONDER WHY?

Food has lost its taste
Wine often mocks at me
Paint of my room seem dull
Perhaps I am falling apart too
Everything around is fast paced
Conversations run out with words
Fun is like the length of a vase
Just like smiles without a face
It feels like am getting left behind
Nights have adopted half moons
Days follow steps of the shade
Seems like time hates my dreams
Many times your finger is naked
That, I wonder where my ring is?

SONNET 6: IF MY BABE WAS AN ARTIST

If my was babe was an artist
She would sketch me gazing at her
Laugh in between posing twists
But steal my eye if I was bare
She would draw my present
A young lad standing at a crossroad
With a sign of desperate unload
Imaginary is an uncertain future
If so, she would paint my happiness
Light colors numbered as good days
Heavy ones layering all of life's decays
Come what may varnish this sadness
If my babe was crafted in art
She'd engrave my picture in her heart.

SONNET 7: DOMESTIC VIOLENCE

Let's get wasted keksy
It is weekend fever right?
Meet me at 2 mile oasis
We'll drink rum tonight
Cloth into shorty's and tights
Show adequate skin, will you?
So men may marvel with sighs
But reply as I am your beau
If you stand too close and dance
Then, forget to spare me a kiss
Phone the ambulance in advance
My punches and kicks never miss
Cause of death unknown at a place
Autopsy: accident or domestic violence?

SONNET 8: DEAR LOVE

Harmonize me that tale of affair we had
Let it perform surgery to my ear drums
Like my fingers that caress the IPad
So that this music frisk without harm
If I should endeavor in this moment
Thine sensations be demoted then
Adore me as a listener's ornament
For your voice circles with no end
If ever you cease this unchained flay
Leave me no replying maneuvers
Pensions of regret are saved by the day
Like a wind of lies hooked on stay overs
Rest me the time that we never spent
Never pardon a story with predicament!

SONNET 9: ABSENT STATE

Take me to a place
Where time is freezed
Only mind playing rhythms
Free from me yet tied
We shall convene in secret
Just the two of us alone
Space declaring mutiny
Cynical tour shall shine too
Have me knocked out
Neither in shame
Nor your lust for my falling
But a rise in delusion
Then this thing you aim at isn't
That what I'd intend to grab!

SONNET 10: OLI KOLIM YU SAVE MAN

Taim neim e pairam antap long niuspepa
Peles e wokim bikpela kaikai na sing-sing
Ol femeli e putim moni – koins na pepa
Long salem yu long peles bilong bik-man ting-ting
Tasol namba faiv dei yu winim gol long pipia senis
Wer sigi man e kotim yu long as bilong pis-pis
Yu lukim polis man na silip long pek-pek banis
Long wanem yu nogat wanpla bikpela bis-nis
Yu drin sop wara na kisim liklik skin pen
Papa e kam na rausim yu long dei namba ten
Mama e wari na salem sampla moa koins bilong yu
Bubu e beiten long yu lo gutpla save bilong yu
Yu no harem tok-tok na spak raun long bia gaden
Sapos mi barata bilong yu, bami tok wanem ken?

KANU OREDAE (TOK PISIN)

Solwara e karim nek bilong kanu oredae
Tok bokis bihainim singaut bilong bubu
Ol man e kandis lo em sing-sing na danis
Olsem olgeta kanu ron long baksait kilia tru.

Win ino bin giving sans long ol arapela lain
Em e maretim sel bilong oredae na pilai
Tupela krew e skelim pikinini kanu long sait
Na man e lukautim pull e banisim ron nogat skindai.

Long lastpla mak we ron e sapos long pinis
Fopela kanu e kapsait olsem hap aion
Ol man long holim rop e pinisim gut stong
Tasol hevi e karamapim biksot tintin na sem.

Oredae e tanim kona na makim ples nambis
Bubu man e mekim luksave na hapim han kais
Ol anti e pairapim sos pan na ankol e paitim kundu
Bilong wanem, nek bilong kanu
E kam sua pinis long haus dua.

Vagi Samuel Jnr.

A Canoe Named Oredae (English Translation)

The waves of the sea cherished
The voice of our canoe, Oredae
Parables echoed about my grandfather's words
To all men that gambled at its delight
They sang and danced
For a race as such painted all canoe's in the backdrop.

Winds from the east never bargained with the other racers
It married the sail of Oredae
And lead on the rest of the play
Two of its crew pendulum on its small hull,
Tamed on the west
As the skipper anchored the rudder
Without the faintest of pain.

Upon the last leg of the course
Where the end was to be a cruise
Four canoes submerged like the demise
Of a small piece of metal
Where the crews failed to fasten
Intertwining ropes at all ends
Their sails could not afford the swing as pride
And shame turned.

Oredae at a glance turned toward the village beach
My grandfather in elation
Threw his fists into the innocent air
My aunties stoning the tanned pans
With uncle's pulsing the *kundu*
For the voice of our canoe has arrived again
Once more at the door.

SAPOS YU BIN TOK (TOK PISIN)

Liklik taim tasol mi tupela e bin raun
Long namel bilong sem na poret
Taim e bin banisim mi long tokim yu stret
Olosem yu wanpla bikepla pes lo taun.

Lon kona we yu bin stap planti krismas
Mi no bin burukim kiau lon kamap long haus
Kain kain ting ting mekim het e paul tumas
Long wanem mitupla ino bin bungim maus.

Na sapos laikim bilong yu ibin stron lon mi
A ting mi tu bai salim pasin wantaim nogat moni
Pilins bilong mi tu e karim dei we san e bungim ren
Na nait tu e kisim laip bilong mun we lewa e pen.

Long wanem baimi rausim hevi bilong mitupla
As bliong bugim yu namba wan taim tu mi wari
Sapos yu bin tokim mi long inapim yu wanpla
Mi bilip olsem hamamas bai rausim gut ai wara.

IF YOU HAD SPOKEN (ENGLISH TRANSLATION)

For a little while we had this little tail of love around
Wherein shame and fear had us begin for more
Time had walled me from whispering a folk lore
That of which you have become a celebrity in town.

From the eccentric place you have swollen your growth
Not a time, have I broken innocence to that vicarage?
Many a demanding thoughts have kept me in doubt
For a demeanor have us not lip-locked with courage.

If your passion had synagogue moments about me
Then thoughts about fueling love will not require my money
The feeling I have is like a day making out with the rain
As the night robs the moon,
I succumb to more emotional pain.

For what reason have I to withdraw our hidden laden?
Imagining the glue of love at first sight, I wonder why?
If you had spoken about treating you like a maiden
Then, I believe glee would have sucked
The tears from your eye.

THE RING OF LAKWAHARU (ENGLISH & MOTU)

As Loloata dances with the moonlight tourists
Motupore coats the brains of marine biologists
Before the quiet winds of vea gusts onto Gairemotu
Divers from Gwarumemase repatriate at two.

The plains of Dimairi is greeted by lahudiho
Subtle streams of Mirigeda echoes sentiments
And as Nebo begins her day of logging shipments
Mamala is dressed by the mangroves of Matoagabi.

Nadibada exhales the heat of Kari Kari
The refreshing breath of Gealatana astounds them
Oh, what a feeling? Remarks meekish Kokitoa
From Kobosere to Bisiro Daga-ahu is Lakwaharu.

Then, Mirigini's evening appeal drugs Mirikone's eyes
Before Daromia's re-enactment of the mighty Laurabada
Manunuha whispers her sea prayers
Better off, Sir Buri's Tutu welcomes Lahara with open arms!

SARONI (MOTU)

Hera namona ta
Golo danu rohakauna ta lasi
Reva-reva hereana ta
Kopimu latanai e-heatolasi.

Emu raka amo na-rohakau
Matagu epidia gini tore
Emu kiri regenai do asi nakau
Kudougu hisina be Dohore.

Una hora si-na amo o-guigu
Tanu danu eme marere
Lalomuai lau be so-lalogu
Hemami danu eme kerere.

Oitagu-mu to lau be au ta
Sinavai badinai egaramu
To ani-na ta sehe karamu
Reana hari ma nega ta.

Dia laumo to haida danu
Edia nihi amo e-hekaramu
Emu headavai hari baina hetoni
Badina be oina lau egu saroni.

SHARON (ENGLISH TRANSLATION)

Beauty it is I see
Better than silver or gold
Traditional tattoos unfold
On your skin-seducing me.

The way you walk
Leave my eyes to no shame
The way you laugh, tame
Every heart beat without a knock.

Intermittently, I am bound
By the quake of your stance
In your mind I don't have a chance
I stumble for you make my world go round.

You see me but I am absent
Like a tree beside a river without its sleeves
Forever my roots' bear nothing but grieves
To hold you like a birthday present.

It is not only I that has stared long
Enough to be joined by other men
On your wedding day, I shall part you and
Rejoice! For you were once my Sharon.

SINAGU EH! (MOTU)

Hua taurahani ta emu puse lalonai o beugu
Dina badana ai oha varagu
Emu hisihisi be manoka lasi taruanai
Egu tai regena amo oi o kiri tai.

Ratamu ranuna ai o-ubuguva
Vasiahu namo be bubutau ena reke gwarumedia
Parao kininini be bubuhahine imana gaudia
Egu bogakunu danai so laga ani namonamova.

Lahara ena toa lalonai matagu danu se kapuva
Varo kiapana ta ai o huigu lalokauva
Mahuta lalonai reudu anena danu oabiava
Hereva siri tabe ta lataguai o hadoava.

Egu gorere lalonai o geigu loaloava
Dina siahu bona medu bada lalonai
Kememu kopana ai o taruguva
Hemami namo bada taugu idoinai.

Egu bada oho lalonai o guriguri laiguva
Nega dika herediai danu so hesikuva
Dina namodia iboudia be egu goada roboana
Be emu lalokauna golo hetomana to asi davana.

Hitolo bona ranumase na asi nahuadia
Na laloloumu bona mauri gunadia
Baina hereva to na laga tunamu
Badina be oina lau kudougu biaguna.

Dina danu vada ekwadogimu
Maurimu ai baina hamaoromu
Sinagu E! Oina feiva kori kori
Badina be egu lalokauna hegena ori.

MY MOTHER (ENGLISH TRANSLATION)

For nine moons you carried me in your sack
On that glorious day you bled me out into this world
The pain you bore wasn't in the camp of a softened back
For the sound of my cry made your flickering eyes to melt.

From the milk of your breast I was fed
Residuals from fresh fish netted by grandfather
The Motuan porridge at the gifted hands of grandmother
For my sakes bid you of all people did not rest too well.

From the breath of the easterly winds I could not sleep
Abound in a stringed bag I was laid to where I belong
At the point of my dreaming you melodied an ancient song
Along with words of wisdom that you planted
In my soul so deep.

Through my darkest hour of sickness
I would cling onto your shoulders
Whether it was sunny or encoring rain, you never complained
For the warmth delivered from your cleavage
Was never bargained
Better than sweaters for which I was always named
Amongst shareholders.

Growing up you prayed every single day for my destiny
From bags of shits I brought home you never gave up on me
From plain white deeds I must admit the great I am to be
Is that your love is like gold
Which I cannot buy with my money.

Through hunger and thirst you stood against desolation
I stand here reminiscing about the memoirs of yesterday
Lest to every impending genre of great consolation
For the faintest of idea is the candle that burns every day.

The end of this life is coming very soon
And while you are still alive
I am honored to deliver this message
Oh Mother! You are my hero without a platoon
For my love for you is like the clouds
With a mere silent passage.

IDAU TAU (MOTU)

Bibinagu idau hegera oi bibinamu
Taiagu ena Lalokau oi gadomu
Imagu idau haheura oi gwabemu
Kudougu ena kiri oi hetomamu.

Hereva mamina be idau damena
Kamonai anina danu do sehekara
Emu gori sivaraidia be mamanoka
Lalogu danu seme laloparara.

Be aogwa lau be taina namo?
Lau be lalohadai ta name havaraia
Be aogwa lau be babo?
Egu kava ese Lalokau ea hedinaraia.

Aita nohobou heina hua henunai
Diarina ese huimu do bema papaia
Matagu ena hegausi namo daenai
Niu kodevana do boma hehoro laia.

Emu gwau ai lau be lalokau ta
Toh bamomu vairadia neganai
Lau be idau tau, reana lauma ta
Emu kara dika amo vabura e hanai.

Egu laga oredia na hahodiva lalonai
Una lamepa goadana danu ma e dabuva
Lahi ena hekise maurina baine tarua
Toh guba diarina e ginidae lau kudouguai.

Vagi Samuel Jnr.

JUST ANOTHER MAN (ENGLISH TRANSLATION)

My lips ogle your beautiful lips
My ears rejoice at your sweet voice
My fingers trace the warmth of your hips
My heart smiles like your glowing face.

Your whispers taste like salt
But my feelings are inadequate
Your words to me derail and stall
The sex appeal for us to mate.

Tell me that I am crazy and plain?
I may have freed the bird
Tell me that I am insane?
For love I will be the dirt.

Sit with me under the full moon
Let its light have an affair with your hair
Let the flowers glow and roses bloom
Like the coconut oil that plays with flair.

You say I am your love
Yet I don't exist amongst friends
Perhaps another man, a ghost
Inviting darkness not make amends.

Till the day of my dying breath
The lamps could not even reveal me
I was at the verge of feeling the earth
But heavens glory came to set me free.

TUBUSEREIA (ENGLISH & MOTU)

The savannah plains of the central sleep quietly
Rocked by the cool breeze yelling south-westerly
Her curtains made of white cumulus clouds
Deterring the sunlight attire of the Barakau blouse.

There she sits along the Papuan coastline
Savoring the neat stretch of scenic greens
Past rivers that trench before the borderline
Of the capital, welcomed by nomadic grins.

She sings a song of praise about Lakwaharu!
Traversing through the curves and curls
Aboard the showers of a sailing *Larahara*
Cherished by the pounding beats from her shells.

Oh how she caresses her children by day
Laurabada on a joyous ride along the way
Rough, as Loloata and Lions islands' dream
Of a wonderful evening from *Mirigini's* lean.

She dances with the stars at mid-night
At the soulful swirls of the blue seas voice
As dead-fish island joins in the moon light
Lahu-diho naively applauds without a noise.

Oh how wonderful it is to see bootless bay
As Motupore greets dawn with the emerging sun
Painted by the oceans whispers – a silent say
Wake up everyone, for a new day has begun!

A 15 minute drive off the city of Port Moresby
Awaits this home, at the pedals of a seeker's journey
Turn on the radio and hear the news from the media
She is Tubusereia the origin of Kumul's captain David Mead.

KAIKAI BILONG AI (TOK PISIN)

Taim tingting e save hatim bel
Pasin bilong yu e save smell
Long wanem taim bai yu tanim
Ol kolos bilong na wasim.

Mi ting olsem yu marit pinis
Wer man bilong yu igat bisnis
Na gat fopela pinkini olsem step leda
Tasol yu iangpla yet wantaim lo pepa.

Em orait bai mi sanap luk-luk
Na raitim pas bilong makim dai
Wer het bilong pas bai luk olsem dukduk
Na bami tingim yu olsem kaikai bilong ai.

LAU TUBUGU ENA HEREA TA (MOTU)

Dina ta be ta era bolaomu
Vanagi tuanai tadi badaherea
Ruma irutahuna so itaiamu
Nese danu sisia moi rea
Reke e boimu lau heina
Matamu danu ekapu mase
Gagama madi ehe-mata ah?
Ilapa imana danu do Mauri
Oh, hena asi rahone lasi-lasimu be?

LIMERICK TO AN ABSENT MINDED GIRL

Funny how she doesn't smile
Even when my jokes are wild
I think she's crazy
Or maybe I am lazy
I realized she's absent in mind.

LIMERICK FOR A GIAMAN MERI

Yu salem pas ikam long avinun
Wer bai yumi bung ananit long mun
Tasol yu no soim pes
Na sikin bilong mi les
Yu wanpela giaman meri lo karimun.

LIMERICK FOR A PLES MAN

Poro yu tingim dispela taim tu
Yu mi na meri bilong yu
Em kalap antap long mi
Na yu tingting karangi
Tasol bia kisim em gud tru.

LIMERICK TO A LEADER MAN

He leads his flock by example
Money and pig from him to gamble
Ballot boxes as purchase orders
And policies that cut corners
Just like empty cans that rumble.

LIMERICK ABOUT A POLICE OFFICER

I drive up the highlands highway
You patrol every night and day
I speed and you chase
I stop and you confiscate
My license for what have I to say.

LIMERICK FOR A GHETTO GIRL

I toil the street for bread and butter
I am from the villages called squatter
I work every day
But night has good pay
I smile for I ain't a regular taxpayer!

ODE TO BUBU AMIGO'S BOROGI SINAVAINA

Beneath the green canopies of Borogi
Cries the melodic sound of her tributaries
Pune's whistle through the silent leaves
Descending amongst the whispering trees
And sedates the mind with serenity.

HAIKU: NIGHT STROLL

Beneath the moon light
the waves came crashing ashore
mirigini slept.

HAIKU: AN URBAN VILLAGER

You go to down town
almost every single day
without a wallet.

Vagi Samuel Jnr.

HAIKU: MISSING ANGEL

I like your sweet voice
Heaven is very quiet
Did you fall from sky?

HAIKU: TUBUSEREA BEACHES

Winds howling at it
I hear the whispers rape it
Sad, the black coastline!

HAIKU: SMOKING

We call it Pallmall
A human chimney you see
Arise mist, cancer?

HAIKU: LOVE

You make me laugh loud
Till the sun departs the moon
I wait by the sea!

HAIKU: A SINEBADA

One sinabada
Two I play with in my head
Three misis missing.

HAIKU: BUTIBUM GIRL

Where are you from girl?
Your behind is like a heart
I'm from Beauty Bum!

QUINZAINE: NAKED MIND

I saw her change in the dark
I read the obvious
In a book!

QUINZAINE: PNG MODELS

White is the new dark skin girl
Did she use the bleach?
Mix raced lass!

QUINZAINE: BACK TO FRONT

She wore a laced top that read
Want to date me boy?
Confused Miss!

QUINZAINE: PARTING WAYS

I am the man you ever loved
What made you to flee?
A love bite?

QUINZAINE: COLOR BLIND GUY

Love is the red and white rose
Can you find me one?
Are you blind?

QUINZAINE: A STOLEN HEART

That boy's heart is inside me
Have you asked him yet?
I stole it!

QUINZAINE: LEAVING

You wanted me to go away
Did you miss a date?
Not today!

QUINZAINE: FOR BITCHING ABOUT

This black beach loves the white sand
Can you tell the story?
Are you deaf?

SIJO FOR AGING

Like the ground I came into this world, I was barely clothed
To be dressed today I feel like a breathing soul against time
Wrinkles and smooth head I cannot escape, soon I will be
like dust!

SIJO FOR MAMA AND IAIA

Tamagu,/ dugout a log,/ into a lass/ - Oredae
Sinagu,/ planted biku/ at Sebore/ by the river,/ I sighed
If they never lived,/ we would neither/ sail nor garden/

SIJO FOR DIGICEL CUP

On the field,/ the hype is real/
 as they run to/ gain more meters,/
Crowd cheering,/ they pass the ball/
 dripping with sweat/ at each set play/
In the end,/ the looser complains,/
 referee runs/ for his life!

SIJO FOR UNCLES

My Vava/ I offer you
 Respect and thanks/ for your true grace
That kept me/ from dads thick belt/
 You had my back,/ gave me Big-Boy/
To cheer me,/ I recall at heart
 You stood by me/ at my down.

SIJO FOR A SHARKS FAN

I saw him/ on the green sea
 Drowning raiders,/ hunting broncos/
By the bay,/ a storm stood there/
 Watching panthers,/ strangle the dogs/
His white fin,/ stained by their blood/
 Searching for more, a shark waits.

TANKA: MODERN MODEL

You look like a doll
Under the shimmering lights
On the runway stage
You look like an African
Skin on a skeleton frame.

TANKA: BLOODY TEARS

She sang a love song
Her fingers ran the fifth string
It pierced my empty soul
At the sound of her voice
My eyes bled like bloody tears.

TANKA: WOUNDED FLING

I do not need you
We have to depart ways now
Two roads at the turn
Love without the smiling sun
And hate with the pouring rain.

TANKA: HAVEN'T MET YOU YET

Oh Rose my sweet love
I have never met you yet
But I can feel you inside
I am the man of your dreams
In the wind, silently blowing.

TANKA: FALSE PROPHETS

You tell me to change
Without a woman's taste
To be like a man of worth
I cannot hear what you say
Nor the deeds I see today.

TANKA: LAST BET

You ate bread at school
I ate potato for lunch
You were the brightest
But never went to a varsity
I sit and eat at yacht club.

AMIDST RELATIONSHIPS

As the sun is envious of the moon
A girl feels the same towards her boyfriend
Love hungry and thirsty of obsession
She becomes vulnerable to vulgar and infidelity.

Like the raging sea waves crashing on the shores
A guy is very protective over his female queen
Attention seeking and approval enlightened
He grabs every opportunity to fend off intruders and losers.

As the twinkling stars fall from the night sky
A gay wears possession to gain his lover's needs
Exquisite attire and passionate poses
He uses weapons of seductive manners to satisfy.

Like the cool breeze that blows above the mountain
A husband loves his wife like the sun painting flowers
Pride is the ring, respect and trust being their infinite bond
Love becomes the link until death shall part their life.

INVERSE OF YOU AND ME!

Desperate Lady:
A broken relationship she faces
Is a night bucket filled with tears?
Her heart is burnt, severe head aches
As she tells flashbacks with fear.

She is scared and afraid to love again
But she's focused every step of the way
Frantic guys penetrate with ridicule bargain
As she permeates with a mere silent say.

She feels fresh like a new born baby
It's different with nothing to worry
She's indeed that desperate lady
With the motive for the old to burry.

Confused Guy:
Bizarre is this sweet journey of mine
Turned into a sour situation that is wild
A relationship hoped for long life time
Has been detoured with intentions very mild.

I feel gauche without anger but fear
The absence of courage that I won't marry
Only the indecent proposals I can bear
But the clout of the opposite I must carry.

Partners being honest still can lie
The other envious, one willing to die
Truth is, Love and Trust money cannot buy
That's the reason I am still a confused guy.

DECEITFUL LADY

O that deceitful short fat lady
With immature mind encircling guys
Megalomaniacal freak without friendship
Her lips kissing nothing but fallacious words.

Her second word is using the word boyfriend
Effects of love being turned into hatred plays
That character of hers is a pretending game
Nothing compared to trustworthy and faithfulness.

Thy hate her for what she has become of
Never do I utter my impeccable thoughts
Neither do I shake her filthy hands
For such a loser I have diminished good will.

O you devious and confused girl
Change your ways and turn right
Your folks didn't teach you crap
They blessed you to stay and not to play.

MY VARSITY

A freshman at a University
He walks and talks with glee
Ogling, bluffing without honesty
But there is more than I can see.

Huge ear-muffs, IPod the latest tech
Tire glasses, 50 cent chains tight shirts
Baggy jeans and Colorado's a suiting dress
A first year studying in Lae's out-skirts.

A newbie at the Hetura block
Indulging attire, manicure and pedicure
Modern stature misusing natural pure
Though bright but is tuned in ad-hoc.

Her hair pulled back, ribbon atop
Hooped-earrings, patches of a signature tattoo
Mini shorts with a slanged cleavage white top
Saying "hey dude!" Check me out too!

BEFORE EITHER

To the lips that I am yet to taste
The hands that I am yet to hold
To the flesh that I am yet to heat
The feet that I am yet to walk bare
I know you do just before I meet you.

RELEASE

Deny my eyes even if it kisses yours
I don't mean to be rude
Neither do I intend to be polite
It just seems right to look at you
In a stupid and lucid way
Should you intend to reverse it with a smile?
Then, I suggest you keep it for a while
And walk beside me
Lest we forget this
Monumental moment of release I see,
Otherwise this treats!

DECEMBER LOVE

A ringed woman am I
Traditionally tied
Placed with a subdued duty
Emotionally crazy.

The past revisits me
Ex stares from a distance
What is thee to thou?
Further this caged romance.

Innocent man is hubby
His love shapes mine
Naked whispers deny
As peace parts me behind.

I am surged by this former
Mysterious is tis life
Ex might just be a late-bloomer
Minoring reality that I am already a wife.

December majored deceiving
A month worth chemistrical
Past and present aren't identical
For this reason, it's you I'm leaving.

UNTOLD TOLERANCE

Ironed hair brushed down
Bow clipping thread on top
To thee a smile is sewn
Because her killer was on dope.

Jay picked his blooming rose
As morning glory fell from its source
He ditched his usual doze
Just to have lunch with tomato sauce.

Flirtation strummed an unusual note
She gazed up at his demise nature
Maybe he was the relational antidote
As she played selfie on motion picture.

An unorthodox chemistry
Passing through them both
Patience withdrew from court
As glamour boarded on flight history.

Vagi Samuel Jnr.

FIND ME A LASS

Find me a lass so that I may grow old with
She should be twenty yet two years older
If and when her ways steal my sake's bid
Further, shall my arm be over her shoulder.

Her body shall be mine alone and not others
Like a creeping plant that fences a house
I shall be her guardian if anyone bothers
Neither am I a security for I will be her spouse.

She shall be the mother of my home
Bear me princes' and princesses to behold
So shall we raise a family for years to come
I shall be their father as this journey unfolds.

My youthful status shall be incinerated
Her dignity as attractive lady shall be paid
Come oh dear as our hearts get liberated
Leave your parents and let us get laid.

HER TRIAL

Noble, are her gestures
That bank on luminous deeds
Remnants of her dark world
Begs the forgiveness of thee.

Shall my breathe resist
Neither have I a gasp
Indecent times grips solace
Further thy dirt yonder on.

Peace flirts with distrust
Thus, envious grace sedates
But her wage of manipulation
Hasn't bridged thee's effect.

Shall I not release tis burden?
Or shall I brick the sanity?
Shall I not defend her misery?
Or shall I weaver deception?

The swirling rage of backbiting
Is the door to defame will
Where order misfits revenge
Haven't I a grudge to desist.

I shall wake liberty then
Maybe thy captivity will win
Where her negate flashes
Shall she stand tried to fulfil.

I WAKE UP WITH YOU

I wake up with you staring at me
How splendor it is to be next to you
Your face naturally delivering glee
I keep pleading for this love to be true.

You mean with a whisper of freedom
Into my ears I receive your request
Lead me baby is the words of test
Take my hand arrest be our doom.

I pull your strength from slumber
You desist my zeal with a silent joke
Lay ten seconds please is your poke
My lips find yours free from humor.

We bath purely with a warm shower
Minutes of giggle hates none of us
Sweet is the smell of perfume does
Itchy becomes my heart for an hour.

Near is the direction of our paths
Breakfast own the events last night
We walk out the room with wraths
From Venus merely tis love is a fight!

LAURABADA QUEEN

She is the queen of my society
The tattoos marked on her skin
Tell a story of her noble dignity
Sway darling you make me spin.

Her face is unmasked with a smile
Breasts imitating the *kundu* beat
Her thighs pinching lads so wild
Bare back hails without retreat.

Hoist your clay pot my mistress
Sway till the sun paints you again
Shout to the gods of this sea
Grant us safe passage for us to sail

See her sailing on-board that *lagatoi*
Winds of Gulf chasing her along
Sing and Shout with all your voices
Laurabada's queen is at home!

MAYBE A LITTLE

Maybe a little damp in her hands
Clustered against his shrewd face
A bit of courtesy may have levelled ends
Just a smitch of indignation derail
Have I not secluded your liking?
Many have not known gestures
That I and you have cased striking
But to neither of us this pleasures
Become a sinister come January!

PAYBACK'S A BITCH

Jealousy jumped once more upon him
Every nerve teasing his emotions crazily
His love engulfed by a guy named Tim
As he stood beneath hells ill hopelessly.

Hate began to shower the latter
Fiona as she was known found new love
So she sent an envelope containing a letter
That read: Dear Jim, I am on the move!

Anxiety struck him without due care
His eyes swamped up into its socket
Reading a book titled, 'Why is life unfair?'
As he board on a saddened rocket

Happiness bettered his state at a mini bar
A lass greeted him after an eyeful gesture
Then, he tweeted via his phone to Fiona
I just made love to your sister, Lavender!

SINFUL PLEASURES

Many years apart have we stayed separate?
Our exchange of postcards record numerous
Days of the then flair we had can nominate
Abounding faith that which we feel curious.

For the first time in a long time we meet
Once more perhaps the melody in your voice
Rather seduces my ears so very sweet
Must I not fall for you again, have I a choice?

My offer sailed in on your weakening ego
The little conversation turned into surging
Your heart beat multiplied not to let me go
A reason to ignite passion worth starting.

Pleasing is the vanilla coated lips of you dear
Its taste pardon nothing more than my life
The cleavage of your chest bailed me nearer
Stop! Let yourself drown for you ain't my wife.

A TALE OF LOVE

Love is the easiest part of life
It is soft and can be used but cannot be touched
Love is also the hardest part in life
You can create it but you may find it hard a bit to keep it.

Love is strong in nature but soft at heart
It lives inside of men but dies on the outside
Love has color but it also fades away
It is clean but has dirt when you flirt with it.

Love can fail you but its art is giving hope
It can manipulate you but it gives you its best
Love remains silent but it is not hidden
It will still sprout even if you doubt it.

Love robs your desires but it keeps you intact
It hurts but does take time to heal your wounds
Love creates wounds but doesn't bleed
It breaks your heart but does not even crack a bone.

Love loves hate but doesn't hates hate.

WHEN WE MET!

An evening appeal wove us together
Business as usual about you, me and them
Hours varnish before our arms held each other
As tears from the dimmed sky crashed our plan.

For nights, we didn't harass the mango tree abide the dark
Subdued light from our phones' attended to our communion
Each meeting had the company of mosquito tone in union
Once more eves-dropping teens would sigh at the dog's bark.

Eight months emerged from the encoring
The shape of a basketball re-defined your waist
Everyone pointed fingers at me for point scoring
That got me engaged in traditional bling's at least.

A garden wedding wrapped us a precious little angel
Ours was laughter from each moment of day we dared
Perhaps a life without this gift of love is seldom at an angle
But to us it was the degree of another little life to share.

I MET A MOTUAN QUEEN
To my dearest, Philo R.

In a thousand dreams lie you
Too soon have I chased over
Pulse; please have me not die here
Old as a man's taste to renew.

Seclusion marks tis pity mind
Words depart me in silence
Only have all goodness wind
Apart in a realm of incense.

Thy highness I saw I lifted thee
Couldn't I have waited more?
This longing of like to explore
Swept my boyhood to kneel.

Her pair of glasses once stood
That perfume scent waved a quest
Can you think of my mood?
Or was I to return in haste?

For such beauty etched in her eyes
Pierced mine without hurt
Lest a plea for desire hit twice
A suspense soul who fools with dirt.

Smile me love, beautiful lily
Caress the hums to my ears
Leave me not a trail so bitterly
Come past me tis young years.

Tis love I call forth to win
Isn't the gist of it all?
Nor opinions of man seem tall
Shut! I just met a Motuan queen.

MISTRESS OF SEDUCTION

The quiet night deployed the moon
Town Street as evading as a vent loop
Whispering glimpse of a walking lady
Her figure emerging from a darken ally.

She puffs away in the mystical wet beat
Edge of her smoke burning so intense
A single parent with twists and turns
That welds another grip for body heat.

Pretentious trade relieving an alarm
Tinted car succumbed by her potent top
Lips inking about service fees and plot
Beer! A hundred waits at gorilla farm.

Baby, kiss me not on my swollen pride
Rather this glimmering sensualist tie
Abound tis petite neck cum abduction
Money owns this mistress of seduction.

THE LAST FIVE YEARS

Something mattered to me in primary
Something so special I recall at heart
Something sweeter than morning glory
Something hate would never hurt.

I delighted you with a single question
Two times the very best of my poise
Your head shake ended my quest on
Shame charged at my wounded voice.

Varsity has just begun my destiny
Manhood obliged me into courting
Suppose I have fallen on love's mutiny
I Beth my pulsating life be deserting.

You met me when I came back
Sudden attack bagged you with regret
I played cool so you'd be on track
As you quenched me without neglect.

This beautiful thing we started then
Not borrowed yet old set although
Changed us both pleading aid band
Maybe smoothened all patches though.

Times of bright events add value to me
Late are the sorry days out of tears
You wasted this something for us to be
Old forever now is the last five years.

Something mattered to me in primary
Something so special I recall at heart
Something sweeter than morning glory
Something hate would never hurt.

AS THE TIDE BRINGS HER HOME

Blue it is I see from here
Plain white clouds looming
From the path I stand sheer
Light weight of my heart in
Despair not for my eyes feel
The touch of sky and ocean
As evening breaths fire still
Even as the haze pin notions
Of memory what my love is for
Once more another day ends
As I dream for the tide to bring her ashore!

DEAR CRY, PITY ME!

Her tears kissed the edges of her face
A cry that defended bruises in between a mask
Could she run? Or cheat death in the moment
Where could she have gone? Rain, come already please?

Going over it in her mind
The words of torment evading her, defeating her
Better off the shame on her cheeks
Than giving into complete despair.

She gazed up to the heavens
Pleas of solemn serenity she begged
Half-mast casted a seldom penalty
These wraths of nature could you send comfort please?

Hopelessness swept through her
Desperation claiming its path
Darkness slowly engulfing her, consuming her
Dear cry, pity me and have me not die here then!

WOMAN OF STATURE

From a distance she stands
Beauty isn't seen
Only the shadow of her hair strands
Harvested by the mere thought of a queen.

From her stride along the beach
Pints of sand cascading gently
Only her smile searching for my eyes reach
Beautiful tis moment of melancholy.

She tells a story that I dream to compose
Intelligence isn't a piece
Only the grace of her wisdom to depose
For I am a shooting star yearning to please.

She has the strength of her father
Muscles I do not see
Only tolerance from her poise which matter
For every moment is captured by me.

She is the soul of her mother
Spirited lass in awe
Only the plight of her being a loner
Isn't found in the streets of hoes.

She has one too many agenda
But is built upon principles of grandeur
Not only does she cook and clean
Add a degree or not, she can write and read.

She sits on a chair waiting for his groom
Not a gentleman from her dream
But vague images etched into the doom
Harbored by memory, in another realm.

Alas, she stands before a mirror
Motions of characters at play, transitioning
From a far and near little voices singing
She sighs come home, my man of caliber.

MEET ME IN MIND

I carved the edges of her contouring waist
My palms shaking to the heat from her skin
Her guise tempting about a starving teen
As I muted her lips with no time to waste.

This moment was not reeling enough
She begged me from the softness of her persona
Perhaps as a Don Juan or Casanova
For the touch she felt made her to laugh.

We did chase the dreams of nothingness
Day to a night would my mind incarnate
Her dawn was like the aging of stillness
That each time we met we would replicate.

We were innocent as romance forged us
Brave young lovers beneath subliminal abstracts
Teasing distrust to the melodies of toiling mast
That which we embodied befalling extracts.

We cried together like rain healing dry cracks
We smiled at each other as if it were out last
We held hands to the memories of our past
We never did and never had as we made tracks.

Meet me in my mind once more delicate beauty
Decapitate the affairs of promiscuous epitome
Imaginations shall succumb before a veto of reality
If you are authentic then I beseech your vow to me.

A GHETTO LADY

A mini skirt glued her thighs
Suiting was a black jacket
Dark sun-glasses over her eyes
As her chest nested a necklace.

Her handbag badged Gucci
Not even a thousand it carries
In it are dozens of make up
Where men are pulled with.

A hooker paving the streets
The pride of her beauty adores
In a cage of family needs
She caresses the survival trend.

To the eyes of the idle public
Her worth is a man's pants
But to the ghetto laureates
She is a treasure to behold.

Maybe the impoverish society
Derails progress to the nation
Rather the policies those are set
Have no value to the agenda.

Despite of the pull factors
She restores the errors in front
Her mandated role to fend
Is a kina note to justify life?

A LOVER'S PAIN

She cries with a broken heart
For she loves her ex very much
Neither does he show nor does he speaks
For he has become a victim without her touch.

She whispers about her internal pains
As he is solemnly the one she trusts
Aches without bruises but sharp inert busts
Only to find herself in tears of pouring rain.

The question is, is he stupid, selfish and ignorant?
Or is he blind, deaf or jest-fully dumb?
Ladies would argue if the guy has an alibi
His interest diverted by possessive tolerance.

He genuinely loved her for her self-giving attitude
But she may have been too obsessed all the more
So he stepped back giving her the whole world
For it drove her mad and she loved her inner sense.

BANQUET OF FORGIVENESS

Dinner thee on a banquet of love
Wherein silverwares mirror passion
Thus, our eyes meet in parallel motion
Even when obscurity tries to disapprove.

We shall feast over a romantic mingle
Begin the old sayings from the end
Our taste renting flames that kindles
That this fumes churn past to mend.

Must we not boast on the finest wine
Not that our drink edges about hate
But let it bury many gist of our whine
Dear to us be memoirs of this date.

Even odds of this table grant elation
Better the loneliness of us depart
To you shall I giveth my lost affection
As tonight is for forgiveness to impart.

HERE I AM

Here I am, my love
Take me and make me your own
Undress me with my robe of guilt
Put on me a fine linen of forgiveness quilt.

Here I am, with my heart
Pierced by the arrow of the cupids dart
Spilling blood of hatred, heal me with your soul
For I am dying because I have been a fool.

Here I am, with my soul
Mate me but befriend others
Be my guest and ride with me with on this foal
A journey that is beyond all boundaries and borders.

Here I am my bride
I stand before you and before God
I take you as my wife
For the life prepared for us by our good Lord.

I AM NOTHING

Beyond my eyes lies infinity
My heart contains love
Yet I am limited by my hands
Even when I feel obliged to speak
My lips are consumed by brick
I wall your warmth and
Hence, I break your heart
But the muscles on your face
Tells me you still want to dine with thee
I am kneed by your presence
Where your tears replenish my fall
You are indeed
An angel
Sent for me
I am nothing.

MARRYING A BRIDE LIKE MUM

Great is her presence
Loving and caring her charisma
Never will be her absence
In my experimenting dilemma.

She is my mother
The one I call for every time
The wife of my father
She looks after me every day and night.

Her fashion is an apron and thong
Wears a perfume of laundry scents
Bears on her heel a mop and rag
Walks like a nomad on the cement.

Patience defines her whole
Love consumes her heart
Tears describe her soul
But looks fine when all is hell.

Her smile is like a mirror
The inverse of my life
My dream of having a wife
Is marrying a bride just like my mother.

MY VALENTINE

Every day our hearts clash
Envy roars without ceasing
Every night we sleep side-ways
As eagerness paves our path.

Love isn't too hard on us
Arguments coat us from fisting
Of which torment bluffs
But laughter smooth tis affair.

Pain punches our faith
Even more it thickens
Sorrow is bagged by losing
But growth is delivered instead.

Lying sure does lock happiness
Even though the looks we read glow
We proclaim our apologies onward
As today grants me, you to be Valentine!

I love you
Happy Valentine's Day.

TINIEST SIN

He lurked beneath the curtains
Defying dust and crawling ants
Serenity became a perfect backdrop
As his eyes robbed of her towel.

His fingers molested the fly-wire
Peeping flawlessly through the tiniest sin
That shower scents from her soft skin
Elevated his senses like a stoned man.

He resisted such a seductive gaze
Sweat dripping, muscle aches in vain
She looked cute as she scanned the wardrobe
Bare! His feelings dressed her up in lingerie.

What is man to deprive himself?
Who is she to lure his innocence?
As a man thinketh
Sin be forgotten instead.

TIS NIGHT OVER

Men fish the bar
Butt on the iron stools
Value paper the bench
As rum-shots cream them.

Mood air the business
Talk HR, Sales & Marketing
Ideas breed & cards turned
Blue Winfield clears the slate.

Ladies insulate the club
Pouched by cushioned seats
Jewelries light-up the scene
As glasses empty a bottle of red wine.

Career agenda light up
A partner, Lawyer & Banker
Dating scores par the night
As flirt depart them all.

A FLORIST CONFESSION

In my teens I have had gardens of many plants
Most of which I liked have become well nourished
Others which I have not have become malnourished.

Now I dig so hard to replant
Even though I try my luck seems to run dry
In a matter of months they would be burnt
But my heart told me not to cry.

Feeling lonely I bought a few more seeds
I buried the whole batch so they could live
Again all died but a leaf emerged to please
Where I had all my time and love to give.

It grew to be my beautiful rose
I watered her with my flirting charms
Fertilized her with my lovable dose
To ease her if I'd show any of my harms.

She blossoms her smile to every time
The petals are her eyes ogling me her innocence
The pores are as her lips giving pure romance
She stands on her stem looking so fine.

Even then
I'll be gladly there
Just to be with her
For every single moment.

I am a Loser

I am a looser
The misery of my own true self
The mystery of an outside skelf
More so with a darkened inner.

The strands of her hair cascaded
Down the blush of her cheeks
Robbing her eyes from my greets
Up the rush came her tweets
But a fleeting entrance was barricaded.

Her ears turned red at my bass voice
The receptive nature of her – in isolation
My beating heart drumming her consolation
Such a melody invading her from indignation
Yet the wall of virtues became her choice.

My hands, clamped the wisp of her persona
Like an iron tracing the patches of attire;
A vast savannah waving in a thunderous fire;
Or like the ocean fare welling a wave to retire
But she just kept that face that read, never!

Then, I realized I am a looser
The misery of my own true self
The mystery of an outside skelf
More so with a darkened inner.

SOMETIMES I THINK OF YOU AND ME

Sometimes I think you are crazy than me
You test my emotions with shits untrue
You fail me with deeds I cannot see
But I bet you do to make me feel blue.

Sometimes I think you are a smart ass
You throw idioms at me that I may wonder
You play sarcastic cues so I can guess
And I think you do coz at least I ain't a loser.

Sometimes I think you are funny as hell
You pretend a topic is zestful so I'll smile
You make me laugh oblivious to tell
And I think you mean so I'll think for a while.

Sometimes I think of a place called Sogeri
We'd chew buai and gaze upon the weather
We'd stroll down to the drive of Purari
And I think you'd far me syncing Josh Turner.

Sometimes I think of the day it rained
You did what most stupid tease don't miss
You had me basking about my ego to reign
And I think you shut me up so we could kiss.

Sometimes I think you'll be a good lawyer
You would read my rights to keep me sober
You would face me modestly as a buffer
And I think you did so I'll call you Loretta.

Sometimes I think I am not good enough
I am a little bit self-righteous on occasions
I am guarded with words that sound tough
You think otherwise with my skillful orations.

Sometimes I think I am obnoxious
I paint my face with ecstatic glows on you
I peel of my sorrow so you'd feel anxious
You think I am a joker but I am one of a few.

Sometimes I dream of you returning
I wait on the pages of my poetry journal
I ink my thoughts seemingly yearning
You think I am a lad just a Schmidt abnormal.

Sometimes you think I am these and that
But I think even if you do I don't regret
For it's a matter of time we shall meet albeit.

SOMETIMES I WONDER TOO
Written by Loretta Maria Fainame

Sometimes I wonder of a time not distant
A time where reality was as simple as one plus one
When simplicity was a nice afternoon
In the company of a mirrored soul
Not pretentious, not agitated but rather well suited.

T'was always based on intellectual debates
And mostly failed attempts to influence your thinking
Most of the times I think I succeeded
Or maybe you just let me think that.

It was a time when meaningless walks
Meant a glance into your world
A time when a discovery of self-did eventuate
Looking back you influenced me on a little more than I let on
I would dote on your type of music without fully realizing
How much a part of me it became.

On how I'd be singing Josh Turner for hours on end
You thought I was a tease
And stepped up to challenge me regardless
Oh how I'd offend you at times.

But your sunny nature was my ray of hope
You'd have me smiling like an idiot
Sometimes you'd laugh at my jokes
Just out of kindness now that I think of it.

"Our buai sesh" as I called it
Was the highlight of my days
Sometimes I think of that night we met
How I felt I knew you forever.

Or that one time I persuaded a walk in rain

Where boots were simply ignored
The water was above the knee
And I was practically running.

I put you in your place
And you tried your best to shield me from the pouring rain
Still I wonder when I'll get to see that poetry journal
Or if it'll still be in existence when we meet again.

Maybe not now, maybe later
Until then you'll always be my biggest challenge.

GLORY I SEE YOU

Where there is silence
Your laughter echoes
Sweet sounds in traverse
Another one, hissing pores
Gracious an alluring presence
Crickets clapping at evening
Dogs' woofing, barking me sense
Glory, I see you not leaving
Hello! Beauty in the dark
I can hear you.

I KNOW AM NOT ALONE

I knew I had been there
I heard it all from the start
I remember that sultry voice
A soaked up turn of events.

I was a little bit upbeat about you
I was glued to the speakers
Maybe a little bit righteous
I faded amongst the calamity of this place.

I searched but couldn't see
I shouted but couldn't hear back
I dropped on my knees and cried
I knew there and then that I had to return.

I now know that am not alone!

I QUESTION WHY

You are the mirror of your mum
The smile that evaporates harm
You are the pearl lace on her neck
The shining star abide the black
You echo her voice in the void
The silent whispers in my toil
You smell like the garden of roses
The kiss of the sun that closes
My eyes not to see your beauty
The dream of the moons mutiny
Your lips stained with caramel
Like the coffee I sip to repel
Your seductive looks that kill
My morning gaze in thought, still
I imagine the time to say goodbye
To you I question why?

KINGS OF THE FISH, SERVANTS OF THE SEA: A SENEMAI TRADITION

(A mixture of prose and poetry about a young man and his friends going fishing with a veteran skipper, dedicated to Uncle James, Moale, Siapo, John and Rima).

We gathered the fishing nets and folded them neatly like clothes. We took the paddles and pegs, carried them onto the canoe and emptied the hulls with a cut-off four litre container.

Our skipper lifted the container filled with salt water, sipped a little, then faced the east and listened to the invisible wind.

Thereafter, he looked at the sun's eye and shadowed his forehead with his hands before getting on his knees and whispering a fishing prayer, made loud in the stillness of time. *"Galeva!"* he said. A crew of four males, we headed to the ocean like leaving home for war somewhere far away.
She was beautiful with her skin in white and red stripes caressing each pleasing wave. *Oredae*, her name, rocking on the sea like a mother swaying her baby in a *bilum*.

We paddled and sang choruses of the old men's fishing tales as the birds of the sky glided and fussed overhead.

We were kings of the fish but somehow servants of the sea, for the winds carried our spirits at the forefront. We journeyed along Bootless Bay and sighted the ever-smiling Loloata resting in its white sandy beaches and its sailing machines silent by the jetty. It was wonderful.

We arrived at the site just as the sun had tilted. Oh, our skipper, his five senses at work along with fine judgment, mother nature's gift to man, looked at the clear blue sea and quietly said this is it, this is the place.

We tied the floaters to either end of the net and planted sets into the sea whilst the skipper engineered the right positions with light paddling. We could hear the leads bumping as they hit the sandy bottom below.

We silently echoed words of harvest with each passing set. Our hands were like conveyor belts switched on without question. And if the net slightly, accidently tangled, it was soon restored by a verbal bashing from the skipper.

We travelled 200 meters before dropping the last floater. The weather remained fine, home was not in sight but, immersed in our task, we had no reason to look back. This was a fishing trip not a playful matter where we could exercise our mischief at our own discretion. These were worthy moments I treasured with the skipper.

From the last floater, we continued onward with occasional sudden splashes on the sea from the long peg. With our hands and paddles, we made drumming beats on the floor of *Oredae.*

At each splash, the skipper would call out the phrase *"Ah, Galeva ena kara!"* [Oh, Galeva's deeds like these!]. He would repeat this three or four times depending on the response of the waves. It was as if the sea was speaking to the skipper.

Soon after, we started to pull back from where the last floater had been placed. It was a three-man job, so we would take turns at each fifty meters as continuous bending would result in severe back pain.

The moment the first fish was sighted, we rejoiced by calling its name. How beautiful was it to see the colors emerging from the dark water. We whistled and made noises as each catch bade farewell to its home.

In that moment we would converse but still pay careful attention to the net. If a set was hooked by an object, stone or coral, a diver was needed. Each of us looked at each to consider who might err and commit this nerve-wracking blunder. We were so damn scared that it failed to occur.

Travelling back home was the best part of the trip. We carefully removed the fish from the net and placed them into the dug-out.

Just before we reached the bay, we stopped to clean the nets. Whilst doing this, we listened to the skipper delivering the laws and traditions and meanings of our fishing heritage.

By the time we arrived home, the sight of those who came to the garden with our grandparents granted us more happiness.

Now the fish went straight to the fireplace to join the tapioca and bananas from the garden. It was not long before the smoked fish got married to our taste buds. I recall, I so clearly remember, this Senemai tradition.

ABOUT THE AUTHOR

Vagi Samuel Jnr. was born on March 3, 1986 in Port Moresby. He comes from Tubusereia village, Central Province, Papua New Guinea. He has a Bachelor in Commerce (Management) degree from the Papua New Guinea University of Technology.

He loves writing poetry as a hobby. Most of his poems were published in The National newspaper and on online platforms such as Keith Jackson & Friends: PNG Attitude and Poem Hunters.

Vagi Samuel Jnr. currently lives and works in Lae, Morobe Province, Papua New Guinea.

Vagi Samuel Jnr.

www.ingramcontent.com/pod-product-compliance
Lightning Source LLC
Chambersburg PA
CBHW052107090426
42741CB00009B/1706